BE A
CHEERFUL
GIVER

Unlock The Promises of God Through Giving

Cynthia Dickens

Be A Cheerful Giver!
Unlock the Promises of God through Giving Based on Godly Principles

ISBN: 1481859854
EAN-13: 9781481859851

ACKNOWLEDGMENTS

Special thanks go to:

God, who has been there for me and who has never left me. My mother, family, friends, and ministries who have helped shape who I am. My undercover editors—you know who you are—who graciously gave suggestions and feedback. My testimonial friends and thank you so much for sharing! My Promotional Director, Deborah Hanna aka "Snoopy" who jumped onboard from the start, believed in this project, and told me it was *hot!* To DL, my attorney, I would like to thank you for viewing my documents.

I would like to take this opportunity to express my sincerest gratitude to my pastor who spoke with me about sharing my testimony and to Saulie for producing my testimony which resulted in my writing this book.

May God bless each of you abundantly!

Table of Contents

Introduction

Chapter 1 – 1
What Is Tithing?

Chapter 2 – 5
Why Do I Pay Tithes?

Chapter 3 – 9
Why Do I Sow?

Chapter 4 – 17
Tithing Unlocks Blessings

Chapter 5 – 27
Give and It Shall Be Given Unto You

Chapter 6 – 29
Tithing is Your First Step to Financial Prosperity: Getting Out of Debt

Chapter 7 – 31
To Whom and Where Do I Sow?

Chapter 8 – 37
Testimonies

Chapter 9- 57
Scriptural References

Prayer. 63
References

INTRODUCTION

Many of you have heard, while attending Sunday services, about paying your tithes and giving offerings. I am sure the thought has run across your mind: *Why do I have to do it?* I had the same question in my youth. I am a Christian, and I have been for many years. I believe as a Christian it is my responsibility to give tithes and offerings. Why, you ask? It is an act of obedience; it is a request made by God since the beginning. I also am aware of the needs of the local church—for example, paying for utilities, paying the mortgage, paying the costs of maintenance and upkeep of the property, meeting payroll, and providing services to the community. It is through our giving that the needs of the church are met.

Some would say, "Tithing applies only to the Old Testament." The Old Testament of the Bible refers more often to tithing than the New Testament, undoubtedly; however, the Scripture is clear when it says, "For I am the Lord, I change not" (Malachi 3:6). The Lord doesn't change, and I don't believe he changed the process of giving. Hebrews 13:8 states, "Jesus Christ is the same yesterday, today, and forever." There is Scripture that lets us know that you cannot separate the New and Old Testaments of the Bible with regard to offering up to God what rightfully belongs to him.

In the Old Testament, animals were offered as sacrifices to God. We know as Christians we no longer have to offer animals as sacrifices, because Jesus was the ultimate sacrifice for our sins. People are quick to say that Jesus did away with the law with regard to tithing, and Paul is quoted as telling the church to sow what is in their hearts and does not reference the ten percent; however, the Bible is clear, and again, God hasn't changed. Some people believe tithing was for Jewish customs only before Christ. Jews still tithe 10 to 20 percent of their earnings to charity and to their local synagogues (www.jewfaq.org/tzedakah.htm).

Unlocking heaven's blessing is not just for Christians, and the law of reaping and sowing is in effect no matter who you are. The Bible is clear when it states in Galatians 6:7, "Do not be deceived, God is not mocked; for whatever a man sows, this he will also reap." For example, when you are nice to people, people will be nice to you; if you are mean to people, people will be mean to you; if you use people, people will use you; when you sow financially, financially you will be blessed. It is just that simple. Everything in creation comes from a seed, and there is something marvelous in the sight of God with regard to sowing seeds. From a seed, a single stalk arises that will reach from two feet to nearly twenty feet, depending on the growing conditions. It is amazing to me the action of planting a seed of wheat, rice, and corn can produce abundance.

When it comes to tithing, most people will say, "I can't afford to pay tithes." "If I pay tithes, how will I pay my bills?" You may have said, "I don't make enough money to pay tithes." "How can I pay tithes on my current salary?" I am sure similar thoughts are going through your mind right now.

I have heard and seen people feel that giving money is difficult and hard to do. I honestly believe that giving is the key to unlocking the kingdom of God. I am not sure why people find it so hard to give to God. The government will take taxes off the top from our paychecks, and we have to pay taxes on goods and services. We will give tips of 15 to 20 percent to waiters, hairstylists, and spa attendants. We are forced to buy car insurance or else be in violation of the law or be financially exposed in the event of an accident. The secular world is going to get its money no matter what. However, it appears that giving tithes and offerings is a struggle for many. In Matthew 20:22–25, Jesus said, "Give to Caesar what is Caesar's, and to God what is God's."

We hear the pastors of our local churches preach and teach on tithing and giving offerings. I often think, *Wow, this is such an easy concept,* and perhaps it is easy to me because I was taught about tithing in my youth. I would encourage parents to teach their children early in life about giving so that they do not struggle with it when they become adults.

Please understand that I know there are some people who financially can't afford to pay tithes because of debt, lack of job opportunities, and bills. However, I want you to know you can't afford not to tithe or give financially. Tithing and giving offerings for me has released financial blessings, promotions, and unmerited favor (acts of kindness from others) in the atmosphere that has caused me to be blessed. You will reap what you sow! I believe whoever brings blessings to others will see the seeds they sowed grow and will therefore be blessed. All the tithes of the land belong to the Lord, which means everything we own belongs to God. This Scripture is clear when it states, "And all the tithe of the land, whether of the seed of the land, or of the fruit of the tree, is the Lord's: it is holy unto the Lord" (Leviticus 27:30).

My prayer is that you will be able to relate to my story and begin to give to your local church to begin to build and advance the kingdom of God. You can also offer your services, giving time to the local church or volunteering. Perhaps you have clothes you could give away. God requires you to give a tenth of what he has given you so that he can continue to bless you abundantly.

chapter 1
What Is Tithing?

Tithing is ten percent paid as a contribution to a religious organization. Tithes are normally voluntary and paid in cash, checks, stocks, etc. (a custom of Jews and Christians - orthodoxwiki.org).

Tithing is walking in faith that you are going to give to God 10 percent of your earnings—which is already his because everything belongs to God, and what you have was given to you by God. If you really understand the concept and have faith, God continues to bless and take care of you. I am giving him ten dollars out of a hundred dollars I have earned because I am being obedient to the word of God as 2nd Corinthians 9:7 states, "God loves cheerful givers, not people who give out of necessity or grudgingly." Keep in mind tithing is an act of faith and obedience to God. We owe our lives to him, and he will supply all our needs according to his riches in glory. You should not look for a blessing when you give; however, this is the law of God and therefore the expectation is that God will do what he said he would do, as written in Malachi 3:10: "throw open the floodgates of heaven and pour out so much blessing" to me for my act of obedience. The blessing doesn't always come in the form of money. You must understand God may bless you with health, he may give you a way to solve a long-standing interpersonal conflict, or he may give you an opportunity for higher education for free. You never know what form your blessing will come in.

Tithing and sowing seeds (or giving an offering), whether it is to the local church or charities, is the first step to financial prosperity. The law of sowing and reaping is in effect no matter who you are. For instance, Warren Buffett, Oprah Winfrey, and Bill Gates are representative of those who are billionaire philanthropists; they are the biggest financial givers in the world. Have you ever wondered why their barns are filled with plenty (Proverbs 3:10)? Well, it is because of the amount of money they give each year. Remember this: "Whoever sows sparingly will also reap sparingly, and whoever sows generously will also reap generously" (2 Corinthians 9:6). "Do not be deceived, God is not mocked; for whatever a man sows, this he will also reap" (Galatians 6:7). The Bible says in Proverbs 19:17, "He who is kind to the poor lends to the Lord, and he will reward him for what he has done."

I come from a family of tithers. I would gather that 95 percent of my immediate family members are tithers, and we are a very blessed family—not just in finances, but in health and happiness. When did tithing begin to sink in to my heart? I recall every Sunday reciting Malachi 3:8–12:

"Will a man rob God? Yet you have robbed me," and you say, "How have we robbed thee?" "In tithes and offerings." You are under a curse—the whole nation of you—because you are robbing me. Bring the whole tithe into the storehouse, that there may be food in my house. Test me in this," says the Lord Almighty, "and see if I will not throw open the floodgates of heaven and pour out so much blessing that you will not have room enough for it. And I will rebuke the devourer for your sakes, and he shall not destroy the first of your ground; neither shall your vine cast her fruit before the time in the field," saith the Lord. "All nations shall call you blessed: for ye shall be a delightsome land," saith the Lord of hosts.

One Sunday while driving from church with one of my aunts, I inquired, "What is tithing and why do we have to do it?" She explained, "Tithing is when you give 10 percent of what you earn to God. For instance, if you had one hundred dollars, you would only have to give God ten dollars." I thought, *Ten dollars? Is this all I have to give, and I am able to keep ninety dollars?* I was so elated by her response I said, "I can't wait to get a job so that I can give God 10 percent." Imagine how I must have felt thinking, God only wanted 10 percent...that was a bargain to me. It doesn't matter to God what you earn, it's 10 percent for *every Christian*; we have all been tasked to give the same percentage no matter what we earn.

I was speaking with Danny, a friend of mine who agrees with me that children should be taught early on about giving and he told me a story about his son. A little background on Danny, he teaches tithing at his local church, and he teaches members to start with a small percentage of giving and gradually increasing as they build their faith in tithing. Which I thought was great. He told me he taught his children early about tithing and one Sunday his teenage son had to work and had forgot to give Danny his tithes. They were chatting during the week and his son handed him an envelope and Danny asked, "What is this?" His son explained that he had held the money and wanted to ensure his dad put the money in the offering. I thought to myself how honorable? Most adults would find holding their tithes for a week or two difficult to do and here you have a teenager who thought nothing of it. I contribute his actions to the teaching he received from his father.

I believe the method my friend uses to teach parishioners tithing could work for people who need to start gradually. Perhaps this is a great way to build up one's faith in giving.

Chapter 2
Why Do I Pay Tithes?

Bring ye all the tithes into the storehouse, that there may be meat in mine house, and prove me now herewith… if I will not open you the windows of heaven, and pour you out a blessing, that there shall not be room enough to receive it. Malachi 3:10.

Tithing goes back to Genesis as a form of the first act of worship of God by Abel and Cain. In Hebrews 11:4 the Scripture reads, "By faith Abel offered God a better sacrifice than Cain." God instructed them both on what to bring, as he has instructed us. Abel brought his offering, the fat portions from some of the firstborn of his flock. He came with the best. God has not changed; he is the same today, yesterday, and forevermore, and looks for our best to him (Hebrews 13:8).

Tithing is giving back to God a portion of what is already his to begin with, but it doesn't stop there. Tithing requires humility, because it expresses dependency on the sovereignty and faithfulness of God. By setting aside the first fruits of our finances, we Christians are saying, "I give this to you as an act of faith and obedience because I know that my provisions come from you alone."

Tithing shouldn't be a second thought or reaction. When God gave us his best, his son, to die on the cross for our sins, it wasn't a second thought. It was pure *love*. We owe our lives to God for his son Jesus and everything that we have to him. I know there is no way I would I be here if it were not for God's hands on my life. I am nothing without him.

If you want to see God move in your life, give your best, and the word is clear as he promises to bless us as we faithfully pay our tithes and offerings. The blessings we have been promised are both material and spiritual. If we give willingly, our Heavenly Father will help us by providing for our daily needs of food, clothing, and shelter.

I believe when we give generously to people, the ministry, and charities, God is behind the scene orchestrating the blessings we will receive and are receiving because of our acts of obedience. Giving produces harvest to the giver.

Tithing and giving are lifestyles, and these actions should start early in your life. I encourage you, if you have children, to teach them how to be givers and teach them these principles. I was so excited when I received my check, and with that first check I gave 10 percent, and it felt great! I think back over my life, and I don't really recall a time when God has not supplied all my needs. I recall a time when I was younger, and nobody was working in our household; however, we never lacked, and all bills were paid—thank God! I recall quoting a Scripture during that time from John 14:1–2: "Let not your heart be troubled. Believe in God; believe also in me. In my Father's house are many mansions," and also paraphrasing Luke 17:6: If I had faith the size of a mustard seed I could say to the mountain, "Be removed," and ask anything in his name and he would do it.

Do I Tithe on My Gross or Net?

The word says in Exodus 23:16, "The tithe is the first fruits of our increase." First fruit was a Jewish feast held in the early spring at the beginning of the grain harvest. It was observed on the second day of the Feast of Unleavened Bread. First fruit was a time of thanksgiving for God's provision. It was a way of thanking God for all that he has done. I know some would say, "That is in the Old Testament." However, Paul taught the Corinthian believers to set aside a collection "on the first day of the week" (1 Corinthians 16:2) as an offering of thanksgiving.

I have had this discussion with several people, and the opinions and beliefs vary. I personally tithe off my gross income, which is a person's income before taxes are taken. The Bible doesn't say whether you should tithe from gross or net; however, I would say every believer should pray about whether he or she should tithe on the gross or net income and give what he or she has decided in his or her heart, and it shouldn't be done grudgingly, for the Bible says, "God loves a cheerful giver" (2 Corinthians 9:7).

Benefits of Tithing

Malachi 3:10–12

- God will open the windows of heaven and pour you out a blessing, that there shall not be room enough to receive it.

God will rebuke the devourer for your sakes.

- The devourer shall not destroy the fruits of your ground.

- Neither shall your vine cast her fruit before the time in the field, saith the Lord of hosts.

- All nations shall call you blessed.

chapter 3
Why Do I Sow?

He who is kind to the poor lends to the LORD, and he will reward him for what he has done. Proverbs 19:17

The idea that God will ensure your needs are met because you have given to the poor is awesome. Sowing and reaping is a spiritual law that God uses to provide for people, and giving is a form of sowing. The more we sow the more we will reap. Giving to meet someone's physical need is an expression of sowing.

Tithing is defined as giving 10 percent of your earnings, and sowing or giving is what you do in an act of meeting the needs of someone—whether it is the poor, your family, your pastor, or someone else. When you give it should be cheerful and from the heart.

Is tithing and giving offerings just for Christians? There are a number of corporations and individuals who give to the poor or charities and this type of giving is defined as philanthropy. Webster defines philanthropy as goodwill to fellow men, or an act or gift or support by philanthropic funds. For example, donations of money, property, endowment of institutions of learning and hospitals, or by generosity of other socially useful purposes, are some examples of philanthropy. Perhaps the individuals or corporations are not targeting giving 10 percent of their earnings, but a number of these individuals and corporations give more than 10 percent.

I have read a number of articles and I have seen numerous programs regarding how wealthy people give to charities. Warren Buffett, Bill Gates, Oprah Winfrey, and many more are known to be generous to many causes and charities. I am convinced the money they sow comes back on multiple levels.

Bill Gates, founder of Microsoft, is the world's most generous person. "Bill has given away $28 billion so far in 2012. His net worth is about $66 billion. He and his wife have the Bill and Melinda Gates Foundation, which reaches out to the world for a number of causes, such as building better sewage systems for underprivileged areas and spearheading a malaria vaccine clinical trial to fight against a number of infections in other countries" (Forbes, "Gates").

He and his friend Warren Buffett have promised to give away at least half of their net worth during their lifetimes or after they die. Warren Buffett is the current CEO and founder of Berkshire Hathaway. His net worth is $46 billion. He has given over $8.3 billion in donations, and $1.5 billion went to the Gates Foundation (Forbes, "Buffett"). Gates and Buffett started an organization called the Giving Pledge (www. givingpledge.org). According to the Giving Pledge website, they have recruited and signed up sixty-nine of the world's wealthiest people who have promised to give away at least half of their net worth during their lifetimes or after they die—pretty amazing! Now imagine Bill Gates is worth $66 billion and has given away $28 billion. He has given more than 10 percent of his earnings—no wonder his barns are filled with plenty.

In 2006, Warren Buffett made a commitment to give all of his Berkshire Hathaway stock gradually to philanthropic foundations. He is a cheerful giver as he states on the Giving Pledge website: "I couldn't be happier with that decision." His first pledge is to give 99 percent of his wealth to philanthropy during his lifetime or at death.

We all know how much Oprah Winfrey likes to give. She has given away her favorite things, opened a school for girls, remodeled houses of guests from her show, and given away money. Oprah's net worth is $2.7 billion, and she has in her lifetime given about $400 million (Forbes, "Winfrey").

Oprah's level of giving has a two-prong approach in that she gives money and endorsements. She hasn't given as much financially as Bill Gates and Warren Buffett; however, her endorsements of products and books have generated millions for small business owners and people. According to an online article from CNBC, Oprah's talk show was the highest rated program of its kind in television history, with an estimated 44 million U.S. viewers a week. Because of her large following, product endorsements by Oprah have had an extraordinary impact from a career and financial perspective. She used her book club as a platform to help launch books for many writers that went on to the best sellers lists. (CNBC, "Oprah Effect").

Oprah's endorsements of Spanx, a shapewear for women, helped make the Spanx Company $350 million in retail sales. An endorsement from Oprah can suddenly turn a small, unprofitable business into a multimillion dollar company (Investopedia, "Oprah Effect").

Other examples of Oprah's "Favorite Things:"

- Kindle—Amazon's electronic reading device sold out during the 2008 holiday season after Oprah introduced the device and gave viewers a discount code.

- We Take The Cake—A bakery on the verge of bankruptcy in 2004, Oprah's mention of the company helped them to sales of over $1 million a year.

- Carol's Daughter—Once a flea market merchant, Lisa Price has turned the Carol's Daughter line of fragrances into a multimillion dollar business after an appearance on *Oprah*[1].

She has helped launched the careers of many people such as Dr. Phil, Dr. Oz, and Rachael Ray. All three have launched their own shows: *The Dr. Phil Show*, *Dr. Oz*, and the *Rachael Ray Show*. These three have certainly seen benefits of the Oprah endorsement. No one has seen "the Oprah effect" as much as President Barack Obama, whom she endorsed and who won his first bid for the White House in 2008[2]. As you can see, having an endorsement from Oprah can change one's life.

---

1 Ibid., Investopedia, "Oprah Effect"
2 Ibid., Investopedia, "Oprah Effect"

I know some of you reading this would probably say, "They have it to give!" However, they don't have to give. They give because this is what they have chosen to do. Warren Buffett is quoted as saying, "To do good will make you feel good and give you some perspective on life as well." There are ways to give back to others. We can give back to others although we are on budgets, in other ways as I mentioned earlier, by donating clothing, time, and food, among other things.

Forbes has a list of "The World's Biggest Givers." A May 2011 article states that the most generous philanthropists gave above 20 percent of their earnings. One could say they have it to give. When you are talking about giving away billions of dollars, however, that is a lot of money, no matter how you view it.

Based on a survey by *The Chronicles of Philanthropy*, charitable giving by America's biggest companies totaled "$4.9 billion in 2011—companies gave from $100 million to over $3 billion in cash and products combined" (Philanthropy, "Corporate Giving"). The companies that gave to charities, food banks, and other causes are Wal-Mart, Pfizer, Oracle, Merck, Citigroup, Goldman Sachs, and Exxon, as well as others. As you can see, besides individuals contributing to charities and other causes, companies are also giving high donations as well.

You can also play a part in giving. You can give money to your local church or charities. You can help in feeding the homeless, volunteering at the local church, or volunteering at nonprofits organizations. Remember God's word says, "He who is kind to the poor lends to the LORD, and he will reward him for what he has done" (Proverbs 19:17). God is going to reward your kindness.

God will supply your needs, and I know he has supplied mine. Philippians 4:19 says that Paul told the church that God would meet all their needs because they met his needs. This is another example of sowing and reaping in action.

Sowing and reaping applies to anything and everything. You sow love and kindness, and you will reap love and kindness. If you sow wickedness, you undoubtedly will reap wickedness. What you sow you will reap.

It is my belief that when a minister—or anybody for that matter—sows into my life a word or a deed that is life changing, I will in return sow into their lives. My prayer is they will reap blessings for sowing into me. I also believe that our churches should be sowing into missionary organizations or other ministries that are doing things that smaller local churches can't do with regard to spreading the gospel.

Benefits of Sowing and Giving

2 Corinthians 9:6

The point is this: whoever sows sparingly will also reap sparingly, and whoever sows bountifully will also reap bountifully.

Galatians 6:7

Do not be deceived: God is not mocked, for whatever one sows that will he also reap.

Ecclesiastes 11:6

In the morning sow your seed, and at evening withhold not your hand, for you do not know which will prosper, this or that, or whether both alike will be good.

Luke 8:15

As for that in the good soil, they are those who, hearing the word, hold it fast in an honest and good heart, and bear fruit with patience.

Genesis 26:12

And Isaac sowed in that land and reaped in the same year a hundredfold. The Lord blessed him.

Proverbs 11:24–25

One gives freely, yet grows all the richer; another withholds what he should give, and only suffers want. Whoever brings blessing will be enriched, and one who waters will himself be watered.

chapter 4
Tithing Unlocks Blessings

They overcame him by the word of their testimony. Revelation 12:11

This chapter will give you insight into my life and how I attribute my education, job promotions, financial increases, and property purchases to tithing and giving. Every step I have made has been orchestrated by God, in my opinion. Now there have been times where I have veered off into another direction, my fault.

When I began working in health care, as a secretary at a hospital on Chicago's west side, I knew I was headed upward. I began working at the hospital after attending junior college and was very excited to have been afforded the opportunity. While working at this hospital, I met some great people. Charles, the human resources manager at the time, is one of the people who would help me with my career aspirations. He mentored me and gave me advice on what I needed to do to develop in my career. I knew I needed to advance in my career, and I certainly was open to any feedback and guidance Charles would give me.

One day while driving in to work, I began to think about my next move. I began to do some research on other hospitals in Chicago and began to pursue other opportunities. I finally found an opportunity at a university teaching hospital, which is well known throughout the Chicagoland. My initial thoughts were if I could land a job at this hospital, which offered tuition remission (free education); I could pursue my undergraduate degree. I applied for and was offered an opportunity by Betty, the human resources manager, whom I had met years ago and who had helped me previously with another opportunity. Betty would be another great resource and career advisor for me. She encouraged me on my first day of employment to enroll at the university, and I did. I was so grateful to have been given an opportunity to work at this hospital as well as pursue a higher education.

I believe tithing not only can manifest financial blessings, but it also can open up other doors and opportunities for people. I have been afforded some great opportunities, and wanted to explain that I honestly believe my giving played a significant role in my being able to complete my bachelor's and master's degrees at a well-known private university in Chicago for free. God has blessed me in a number of non financial ways and I attribute this to my giving.

There were so many opportunities to move up at this hospital, and I took advantage of every opportunity. After being in the HR coordinator role for fifteen months, I began to pursue other jobs and was promoted shortly thereafter to a position in the graduate school of HR on the university side of the business. My promotions began to be consistent here and I knew I had been blessed!

My Life Transitions

Now, don't think my life has been all happy times. My life became a little complicated. While working and pursuing my master's degree, I began to start to think about purchasing a condominium, and at the time my salary was about $30,000 a year. I had saved enough money for a down payment and began to look for a condo.

I hired a realtor, Lynn, who told me, "I will find your condo today," which was on a Saturday. We viewed about six units, and the last unit on the list was the one I purchased. I found a one-bedroom condo for the miraculous price of $45,000. This condo was huge! I had certainly found a great place and believed it was straight from heaven!

Things were going well for me, right? No, I met a guy, and I got married. I will say it was one of the most difficult experiences of my life, and it brought me to another level in my relationship with God. I was newly married and still pursing my master's degree. I was married to someone who did not tithe and who was the total opposite from me in this crucial area of my life. We started to have major problems financially. I was emotionally drained from other aspects of the marriage, which was deteriorating, and unfortunately the marriage ended in divorce. Now, don't think I didn't want to hang in there. Of course I did. Life just sometimes has a way of throwing you some blows.

I was still in graduate school, working full time, and divorced. I felt a great deal of stress and depression. You name it, and I felt it. I was about $15,000 in debt. I was drowning financially, but I never once thought about not tithing during all of my financial issues. I was the one who was responsible for the debt. Why would I stop tithing?

I sat in my house many days and nights wondering how I was going to make it. I felt like I was literally living paycheck to paycheck, now this only lasted about a month. I kept pushing, praying, and studying; I knew if I kept the faith, things would change for me, and it would not always be like this. I believed with all my heart that life would get better for me.

Things Begin to Change

I prayed nightly to God to help me pay off my car so that I could make it financially. I attended an evening service at a local church in Chicago, and the visiting minister said, "Sow $135," and I was so desperate for a blessing that I wrote a check for the amount requested. I needed God in a bad way.

I promise, God moved quickly and blessed me with two angels who were my coworkers at the time. These two individuals mentored, coached, and guided me throughout my years attending undergraduate and graduate school while working full time. I worked with these two professors for about seven years, and not only were they my colleagues, but they were my friends.

These two knew I was going through a divorce at the time and struggling financially. There were times when I would go into their offices and just cry uncontrollably because I honestly didn't know if I would make it through the aftereffects of the divorce and finish graduate school. They consistently would push and encourage me, saying, "You can do this," and "Don't give up. You're too close."

I don't even know if they knew at the time how afraid I was about my finances, but in the same week they both blessed me financially, and it was what I needed at that time and during what seemed to be my drought month! God met my needs through these two, and I will never forget them. I am eternally grateful and thankful to God that I can call these two friends.

The blessings continued, and the following week I received a scholarship from General Motors, and I received a great raise! I saw things start to turn around for me. I had prayed to pay off my car so I could live comfortably. I called the finance company for the car payoff information and was told it was $1,350. I thought about the seed I had sown, which coincidentally was $135.00. I was elated, to say the least, that the car payoff was $1,350. What are the chances of those numbers being that similar? I used the money I had received from the scholarship and paid off my car. God honored my request and gave me more than enough.

I finally completed my graduate work the next year and took a great job at a rehabilitation hospital, which is one of the best rehabilitation hospitals in the world—always number one! This place was humbling to me and was exactly what I needed to help me see how fortunate I was in comparison with the patients this hospital assisted, and by allowing me a great opportunity to learn and grow in my field. The patients there had extreme medical conditions from major accidents, strokes, and other illnesses that left them paralyzed or debilitated in some form or another. This place taught me to appreciate my life and where I was.

While at work one day, I was sitting in my office, and I had this feeling that I should begin giving more in my tithes as well as to give an offering. I no longer gave 10 percent, but gave above my usual 10 percent. I believed God would reward me because he knew he could trust me with money. He could trust that the more he gave me, the more I would give. I have always tried to make sure I hear God, and that day in the office it was clear if I wanted things and wanted to progress, I would have to increase in my giving. I have always believed I could have heaven on earth. The Bible says, "Jesus came that we might have life and life more abundantly" (John 10:10). The bible says, "Thy Kingdom come, thy will be done on earth as it is in heaven" (Matthew 6:10). I have heard there is no lack or sickness in heaven and this is what I am banking on down here on earth.

I obeyed God and paid more in my tithes, and I was excited to do it. Within a month, I saw the hand of God move quickly. My boss took me to lunch one day and gave me a 12 percent pay increase. I was shocked, to say the least, and excited! I said to myself, "I am going to give more," and within five months I changed jobs and received a promotion to work as a manager at a managed service company. I received a sign-on bonus, I received a 10 percent increase in salary, and this job came with incentive compensation, meaning yearly bonuses. You know what I did? I increased my tithe percent and my giving.

Job Change

My career at the managed service company was a super blessing. I met some great people there! I reported to a vice president who was also a giver into God's kingdom. I remember saying to Jesus, and writing it down, "Jesus, I want you to supernaturally move in my life and move me up like you did her." I needed him to do it quickly because I felt like I was doing all the right things; I love Jesus! I was giving above what was expected and had this expectation that he would do it. My VP, however, was tithing and giving above and beyond, so I couldn't catch up with her. The closer I got, it seemed, the farther she moved up! We are great friends to this day, and she definitely believes in the power of giving.

I was promoted several times at this company and, as I mentioned earlier, my promotions came within fifteen months to two years. My first promotion was to a senior HR manager, and of course I increased my tithing percentage and my giving. I was promoted again—this time to director—and within a five-year tenure, I had three jobs. When I was promoted to director, I knew I was not making the same amount as my peers; because of my giving, however, I believed God would correct this. We received our merit increases for the year, which came in January, and, to be frank, the increase didn't move the needle on my salary. I was knocking it out of the park and performing at a high level. I had the faith and believed God was going to rectify this. I went to my boss and asked for a raise. Now, keep in mind that we had just received our raises two weeks earlier. I was bold enough to ask, and I got another increase. I was amazed.

I stayed at this company for five years, and I loved working there and learned a lot. However, you have to know when it's your time to move.

Another Job Change

I received a call for a position at a consumer products company in Chicago to be a regional human resources director. Keep in mind this was a lateral job move; however, I received greater responsibility and financial compensation. This position offered a sign-on bonus, a yearly performance bonus, and stock options. Oh boy, I had entered into another realm—stock options! I was at this company about two years, but because of HR changes and the culture I decided to seek opportunities outside the company.

I was speaking with a colleague from the previous managed service company that I worked at with regard to referring a colleague I was presently working with. As I was networking, my friend mentioned an opportunity at a company she was interviewing with and said that this company had another opportunity in Chicago. It was a pharmaceutical company. She gave me the name of the person she was interviewing with, who turned out to be someone I knew. I reached out to this individual to give a reference for the young lady who was interviewing and asked about the opportunity in Chicago. She told me there was an opportunity and to forward my resume, which I did. I was interviewed and hired. This job has been a great opportunity for me and has offered career growth and development.

I increased my tithes and giving frequently. In fact I have heaven right here on earth. You hear people talk about heaven and how they can't wait to get there. Well, I can't either, but I sure desire to eat the good of the land and have best right here on earth.

Chapter 5
Give and It Shall Be Given unto You

Give and it will be given to you. They will pour into your lap a good measure—pressed down, shaken together, and running over. For by your standard of measure it will be measured to you in return. Luke 6:38

I believe so much in giving that I not only give to the local church but to charities, family, and friends. I give in nonfinancial ways that include my time, books, clothes, and any other way that I can be a servant. You shouldn't live your life always expecting to receive if you do not give.

Luke 6:38 states, "Give and it will be given to you." What is your legacy? What are people saying about you, and what will they say about you at your funeral? Who have you helped? I would highly recommend that you join some organization and volunteer your time, especially if you are unable to give like you desire. It is important that you find something to do to give to the community and/or your local church.

I first began to volunteer and sow financially into organizations such as the American Red Cross, LINK Unlimited, Boys and Girls Club, and Fellowship of Christians and Jews. It is very rewarding to give your time as well as resources to the community.

I have learned to sow for the hand of God to move. When I sow financially, I am expecting in return from God to meet my need. I am expecting for God to move on my behalf in a mighty way.

chapter 6
Tithing Is Your First
Step to Financial
Prosperity: Getting out of Debt

Money answers all things. Ecclesiastes 10:19

While I was at the managed service company, I began to focus on getting out of debt. The Bible says in Proverbs 22:7, "The rich rule over the poor and the borrower is the slave of the lender." I believe this is true. There was a time when I was dodging credit card companies that were calling me. I know how stressful it is to feel like you will never catch up and you will always owe the lender. I also know Solomon said in Ecclesiastes 10:19, "Money answereth all things." Amen!

I began to really focus on all the debt I was in and prayed to God for a way of escape. He will make a way of escape for you (1 Corinthian 10:12–14). I began to strategize how I was going to eliminate debt from my life. I started by applying every bonus check and income tax check to my debt. I started paying more than the amount due. It took me five years, but, thank God, I was made free from that bondage. I still use credit cards, but most of the time; I pay them off as soon as I make purchases. I am blessed to have been afforded the opportunities that I have had and currently have. I am focused on Kingdom giving and my Kingdom priorities are first. My prayer is to be the head and not the tail, above always and never beneath, and the lender and not the borrower.

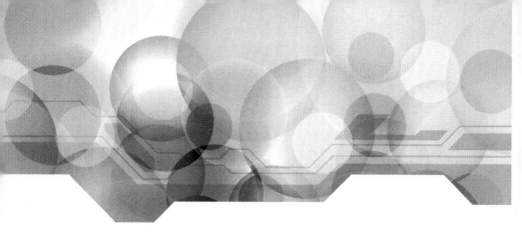

chapter 7
To Whom and Where Do I Sow?

He who sows sparingly will also reap sparingly, and he who sows bountifully will also reap bountifully. 2 Corinthians 9:6–8

Where to Give

There are no rules or formulas about where to give except that you listen to that inner voice inside. As you have read in Chapter 1, tithing is giving 10% of your salary or income to the Lord, which means your local church; whereas sowing is an act of kindness, giving more to either your local church, charities, family, or friends. I would say, however, when it comes to sowing, to give to yourself first and to God. When I say to God, I am meaning to the poor because the poor will always be with us and to give to the poor we lend to God.

Many people are not prepared for a rainy day. I remember my mother telling me back in the day to have at least have $1000 saved. Wow, $1000 isn't very much these days. We need more money in savings in case of emergencies. Some people might say, "Sowing into yourself is being a good financial steward over your money," and that is OK as long as you sow into your bank account. Set aside a certain amount of money for yourself. You should have at least six months of salary saved in the event of a job layoff or an emergency. Set a goal for yourself to begin to save money. Start slowly and begin to increase as you feel comfortable.

Honor your Parents

The Bible says, "Children, obey your parents in the Lord for this is right, Honor your father and mother, which is the first commandment with promise, that it may be well with you and you may live long on earth" (Ephesians 6:1–3). Webster's Dictionary defines honor as "a means to hold in high respect, or revere, one's parents and seeing to their needs."

1 Timothy 5:3 and 5:16 say, "But if anyone does not provide for his own, and especially for those of his household, he has denied the faith and is worse than an unbeliever." Our parents are getting older and will need us to provide for them. Jesus was clear in Matthew 15:4 when He said, "For

God said, 'Honor your father and mother, and anyone who curses his father or mother must be put to death.'" Jesus wasn't playing when he spoke that word.

I honor my mother all the time, and a couple of years ago my mother was looking for a place to live. The rent at the places we inquired about was expensive. We looked for a couple of months. Finally, I thought perhaps I could purchase a place for her to live. I started to look for condos and finally thought I had found one. The condominium complex was seven years old, and the condo was a short sale. I put a bid on the condo for $132,000, but the offer was declined by the bank. I told my mom what happened, and of course she was disappointed.

I received a call from my realtor the following week, and he told me the condo price had dropped to $87,000. I couldn't believe it, but I know it was a miracle that the price dropped. I negotiated an offer of $84,000 with the bank. I know God honored my request because I honored my mother.

I think one of the greatest ways to honor our parents is to provide for them. There will come a time when they cannot work and earn a living. There will come a time when they don't want to go to work but want to relax. There will come a time when they can't do work around the house like they used to. They will simply need help, and the children should be the first avenue for this help.

Your Family and Friends

Acts 4:32–34 says, "The whole congregation of believers was united as one—one heart, one mind." The meaning of this Scripture is the believers shared everything.

You will have family and friends who are in need, and there will be times you may be asked to assist in their time of need. As the above Scripture states, "The congregation shared everything," and the members never murmured about what was theirs. You don't want to be like the person described in Haggai 1:6 as the person who "earneth wages to put it into a bag with holes." Sometimes it will appear you make money and it disappears. You often hear people say, "I don't know where my money has gone." Become a giver, and you will know where your money goes!

I know I have been a blessing to many and in more ways than one. I get joy out of blessing strangers, whether at church, a store, or in a restaurant. There have been times when I knew people who wanted to give and didn't have the money to do so, and I would give them the money. When I saw them again, they would testify that they had found jobs or received promotions.

I receive calls all the time with regard to career advice or help, and I always try to assist people. I have a heart to give and to help people in need, and I love to pay it forward. There have been many people who have been blessings to me. I thank God for my family and for the people who have come into my life whom I have chosen as friends.

Solomon says in Proverbs 11:22–26 that giving induces blessings: "A person who gives freely and does not hoard what he has will be prosperous." Always be prayerful regarding everything you do. "In all thy ways acknowledge God, and He shall direct thy path."

Charities

There are many charitable organizations like the Red Cross, the Boys and Girls Club, food pantries, and the Salvation Army where people can give. Solomon says in Proverbs 28:27, "Be generous to the poor—you'll never go hungry; shut your eyes to their needs, and run a gauntlet of curses."

Jesus said in Luke 6:38, "Give and it will be given to you. A good measure, pressed down, shaken together and running over, will be poured into your lap. For with the measure you use, it will be measured to you."

Volunteer. Do something to help somebody. You cannot just go about your day and do nothing, whether it's volunteering to feed the hungry, clothing someone, tutoring, or mentoring someone at a local community organization. I encourage you to do something. Give from the heart; as the Bible states, "God loves a cheerful giver."

Conclusion

I pray this book blesses you and your family and that you will walk away with an understanding of giving. I have learned that paying tithes and giving offerings to my local church, charities, family, and friends is a testament of how this principle works.

I pray that God will use this book and the Bible to reveal to you the importance of tithing and giving. May God bless you abundantly by supplying all of your desires with his provisions.

chapter 8
Testimonies

I want to share testimonies of very close friends of mine. These are individuals who are prospering, and it is their belief as well as mine that they prosper because of being obedient by paying tithes and giving offerings. We all have our differences in the way we were raised, but there is a common theme among our testimonies, and that is our faith and belief in our God, his son, Jesus, and being guided by the Holy Ghost, who directs all of our paths, along with this strong conviction to tithe and give to local churches and charitable organizations.

Hill

I come from an unchurched background and did not know much about anything related to church. However, I do recall as a young boy when my mom gave me money to put in the offering basket, and, of course, I obeyed. I remember at twelve years old my church pastor approaching me and telling me to start a lawn-mowing business. He bought me my first lawn mower, which was orange, and created fliers for me to pass out in the neighborhood. Who would know that my first career experience would be as an owner of a lawn-service business?

I wish I could say that this gift of business God gave me at the age of twelve escalated into something profitable, but I can't. What I can say is this entrepreneurial gift from God was subverted into a life of sin for the devil, but thanks to God for saving my life and bringing me back to him.

I confessed Jesus as Lord over my life once again at age twenty. I worked a couple of jobs and still did not really grasp the concept of tithing and giving, but I knew I had to give something to the local church. Although I had confessed Jesus as Lord over my life, I had not found a local church to fellowship at, and I wasn't giving tithes and offerings consistently as I should have, but I knew I had to give something. I would get money orders and save them until God would direct me about where he wanted me to give them.

During this time of soul-searching, I worked at two companies. I know that God was with me as I felt this awesome favoritism on my life. It appeared at the two companies I worked for that I had so much favor! For instance, I worked for a hotel for about two years and began as a banquet-setup employee. I worked in this position for about a month, and the supervisor came to me and offered me a job as the night auditor. I was trained as night auditor, and I perfected this role. Within two years, I was promoted to front-desk manager.

I also worked for a company in Urbana, Illinois, that produced car bumpers, and my role was material handler. After doing a great job, I was again promoted to team lead. I had the pleasure of meeting the owner of the billion-dollar company, and I got a lot of inspiration from him. He grew a business with a $16,000 loan and his savings into a billion-dollar company. This is extraordinary! As I looked at this owner and CEO, I thought to myself, "I can do this too," and I left the company and began a real-estate venture, and I finally found a local church in Chicago.

I become a member of this young, growing church in Chicago where the pastor lives what he preaches. I realized that there is more to church than attending and that you have to get involved through volunteering in ministry and by giving financially. I began to understand this concept of tithes and offerings. I totally understand that the unction I had to give was real and that I needed to do more and follow the principles of giving. I remember when God spoke to me about giving a $5,000 seed to the church, and how I wrestled with that, but I did it, and my obedience to the voice of God blessed me. Now, don't misunderstand. I didn't give to get; however, that is the law—that you "reap what you sow." I had it coming to me.

By 2005 my real estate business began to take off, and in January and March of 2006, I bought two pieces of property. One night at Bible study I said to myself, "I am going to sow where I want to be." I increased my tithes and my giving. In 2007, I had a real estate deal that made $40,000. I applied for a line of credit and was given a $50,000 line of credit. I went from owning four units to thirty units in six years. I would describe that as miraculous! What is more miraculous is that half of my portfolio is paid for.

I know my blessing and prosperity are directly attributed to my giving, paying tithes, and sowing seeds. I asked God to show me how to maximize my giving to the local church, and he did. I don't have a safety net; I don't have the higher education and a day-to-day job. All I have are the skills God has given me to make money. I have no other choice but to trust that if I am obedient and give, that I "eat the good of the land."

As I was growing spiritually and as a single man, I knew without question, the woman I would marry would be a tither. I married a woman who is a tither, and she wouldn't have it any other way. One of the first things she asked me was, "Do you tithe?" My wife and I are true believers in tithing and want to teach our children early how to be blessings to the kingdom of God. We have one child currently, and my prayer and desire for him is to know and understand the principles and the way of God. Based upon my past mistakes, I want to build a legacy for my son, so I sow for his future. I want him to get in those circles and have the opportunities that I don't currently have.

My life is dedicated to honoring my family and being a blessing. I honor my mother, and I am always thinking of how I can bless her. My desire is to pay off the house she lives in. I am grateful that I have been able to purchase her a car and other things. I am a servant and have a servant's heart, and I try to help as many people as I can, including tenants who reside in properties I own. I am often giving people a break on rent and purchasing toys for the holidays. My prayer as a young man was not for money. Making money has always been pretty easy for me. Growing up, I never wanted to have my gift perverted, but unfortunately my gift led me into a life of sin. Thanks to my Lord and Savior, Jesus Christ, who has blessed me with all spiritual blessings in all heavenly places in Christ. He has created in me a clean heart and renewed a right spirit in me.

My goals in life are to be debt free, teach other people how to gain wealth, continue to give to the local church and other organizations, and be a good husband to my wife and a good father to my children.

I know tithing and giving offering has been an instrumental part of my life and has afforded me an opportunity to pay for the house I currently live in with cash as well as pay for four other properties in cash in 2011. I know nobody is doing this for me but God. He has put me in the path of people who have entrepreneurial mind-sets and who operate with a spirit of excellence.

I am a member of a ministry that prides itself on excellence. When the ministry makes moves, I make moves. I mimic the moves of the church from a business and professional standpoint. I have learned a lot about being an entrepreneur in the areas of real estate, taxes, maintenance, and construction. There is a lot to having and building a business and I know if it had not been for God in my life directing my steps, I would not be where I am right now. I know it takes great faith to become a consistent tither and giver. I pray through my testimony that you can be blessed, as I have been blessed through my giving.

Nicki

I remember exactly when I thought about tithing, which was in the fall of 1999. This was to be one of the best years of my life with the expected birth of my daughter. Unfortunately, the sudden passing of my godmother six weeks after my daughter's birth made that year challenging. During that year I remember my spirituality beginning to shift. I no longer desired to attend church. However, the Holy Spirit led me to live a righteous life for my daughter's sake. I often tell my friends that becoming a mother saved me. Yes, while in the world I was something else!

In October of 2000, I joined a church that required new members to attend foundation classes which taught about faith, tithing, and being a Christian. I remember not knowing how to pray when I arrived at this church, although I had been in church the past fourteen years. My very first prayer was so simple and consisted of me asking God to help me stop biting my nails. Immediately, I was delivered from nail-biting. I know most of you are thinking, *You wanted to stop biting your nails—that was easy.* As a matter of fact, it was the opposite; I had tried on my own to stop biting my nails for twenty-seven years and failed. Oh, but God. Every time I look at my nails now I instantly smile and think about God's goodness.

Months after being saved, I began tithing. I became frustrated with it at first because I didn't have a permanent job and could give only 10 percent of any income at the time, which was little to nothing. I remember telling my friend when it was giving time that I was embarrassed by giving

$2 or $20 in church, but she quickly reminded me that it was 10 percent of what I had earned, and it's not going to be like this always. Boy was she right! After obtaining a permanent job and making more money, it was hard at first to give 10 percent of my income because I had bills to pay. I was often reminded during my dreams from God that by being obedient and faithful in my tithes he would rebuke the devourer for my sake. As hard as it was to give $200 or more every check, I did it because I trusted in God, and he had taken care of me and my daughter, providing all of our needs from finances to bills being paid and allowing us to live debt free. Now, I must admit over the course of tithing, I backslid maybe three times.

During those times, everything from the car breaking down to problems going on at work to falling behind on bills started to happen in my life. I knew why all those things happened. At no time when I was faithfully tithing did I experience car troubles, work issues, or falling behind on bills. Never again have I missed out on tithing. I remember not attending church for two months due to knee surgery. When I went back to church, I already had my tithe checks written out for those months. God has blessed me enormously financially! I live a debt-free life, all praises due to God! I live according to his word, and God exceeds my expectations with his abundance!

Ann

God's blessing has been upon me my entire life. I grew up seeing my parents pay their tithes, give their offerings, make their pledges to the building fund, and so on. So giving to God and the church has been instilled in me from an early age. When I graduated from high school, I tithed the graduation money that I received. At that time, I started seeing the bountiful blessings that God will provide if you are faithful to him. Fast-forward to my adult life and working in corporate America.

I was working at a company that was experiencing layoffs on a regular basis, like many other Fortune 100 companies. One particular year, I saw the writing on the wall that my job was going to be eliminated. I had been faithful in my giving, so I knew that the Lord would bless me and take care of me. Once I received official notification that my job was eliminated, I wasn't concerned, scared, nervous, or angry. I knew that God had always taken care of me, that I had been faithful to him, and that he in return would continue to be faithful to me—even though I knew I was going to lose my job.

I continued to pay my tithes. Shortly after I received my notice, another opportunity became available—a promotion became available. I did what any person would do who wanted to advance his or her career and remain with his or her current employer: I applied! I went through the selection process and received the promotion, which took me to a more desirable location. I thoroughly enjoyed my new job and the new location. After a little over a year in that job and with my continued tithing, God was preparing another opportunity for me.

I was doing well in my profession. Headhunters and recruiters from companies started contacting me about opportunities within their organizations. These other opportunities were very attractive and would have been promotions. I was in conversations with several companies, but God blocked those opportunities. I didn't understand what was going on, but then calm came over me that let me know something was going to happen. I just needed to be patient and wait, which is what I did. I didn't know how long I would have to wait or what I was waiting for.

Shortly thereafter I heard that a colleague in another location was going to pursue an opportunity that would create a vacancy that would need to be filled. I spoke to my colleague and told him to sow a seed as he pursued the other opportunity, and I would do the same. Unfortunately, the opportunity did not come to fruition. Surprisingly, another opportunity came about that he was interested in and pursued. Yet again, I sowed a seed, and he got the job.

Now an opportunity was present for me to pursue, which I did. This resulted in another promotion in a little over a year. I relocated to a city that I wanted to make my final home. I worked on some amazing large-impact projects and started fulfilling some of my nonwork and more personal goals. I guess what the elders at church said was correct—you can't beat God's giving!

Shirley

I am a tither! I love being a tither—not because I am always looking for something to happen when I tithe, but I do have an expectation that God will pour out a blessing that there shall not be enough room to receive it. Why do I have that expectation? Because God said it in his word— you know the Scripture: Malachi 3:10. Knowing that God always comes through on his word, I have an expectation that he will do just that. Three years ago I took an assignment that required me to travel almost weekly. When I took the assignment, I was aware that it was a three-year assignment only. I had no idea what was going to happen at the end of the three years, as my company could not continue to pay my commuting expenses, and I was not willing to relocate to another state.

To be honest, I wasn't worried at all about what would happen at the end of the three years because I knew God had a plan. A couple of years after taking the assignment, it was announced that my division would be sold. Would you believe the planned closing date was just twelve days past the three-year mark? In other words, when I committed to the three years, I had no idea my division would be sold in three years. This is important because if I had just left my assignment at the end of three years without my division being sold, I would not have been eligible for certain financial bonuses that accompany the sale of a business. God is good!

I had the option of remaining with the buying company, at least for a while. I made the decision that I would prefer to leave and look for a position in my current city since I was not open to continuing to commute. In addition, I still wasn't willing to relocate to remain with the company where I had sixteen years' tenure. When I shared this with people, they gave words of encouragement; however, I could see that they were thinking I was a little nutty. Why would I leave a company where I had many successes, many promotions, and where I already had a certain level of credibility? To top it off—I really loved working for that company and had no complaints regarding my treatment during the time that I was with the company. Was I nervous about finding another job? To be honest—I really wasn't. I was anxious to know what the job would be and asked God for hints from time to time, but I had no concerns that I would be able to find a great job and maintain my current style of living. Without going into too much detail, I found a great job with a great company three months earlier than my planned time frame. I know I said it already, but God is good!

William

My Texas family is from deep in the heart of the Bible Belt South, and we were raised in the Baptist faith. Our pastor, like many Baptist ministers, often delivered the sermon "How has a man robbed God? Yet ye have robbed me in tithes and offerings." Growing up in this church over the years, I heard our pastor preach about tithing 10 percent of your gross income as a means of ensuring you did not rob God and supporting the church's outreach ministries. Listening to this sermon repeatedly over the years, I knew from a Biblical perspective he was correct; however, from a faith perspective of giving 10 percent of my earnings I wasn't emotionally there.

I relocated to the Chicago from Texas in the spring of 1998 for a renewed start personally, professionally, financially, and spiritually. With that move, I also brought along with me a personal debt of $30,000 by age thirty from years of being underpaid and overspending on credit cards in my youthful twenties. Although I was a "tithing" Christian, I fell into the pattern of limiting my tithes and offerings with the mind-set that if I gave a smaller amount that I could spare, like $5 or $10, he would understand and forgive me, so that I could use the remainder of my money to pay monthly expenses and in the futile attempt to pay down revolving debt. For many years, this faulty reasoning kept me under a mountain of debt that could not be moved by my own feeble efforts.

As is often the case when we ignore and/or disobey God's instruction and guidance for our lives, we fail miserably.

During my early years in Chicago, I was in a difficult financial state. The stress of living paycheck to paycheck, month after month, year after year, while trying to figure out how to make ends meet was nerve-racking. Truly enjoying life or feeling that I could purchase items beyond basic necessities was difficult while always having the burdensome, worrisome weight of revolving debt casting a dark shadow over everything I did or wanted to do.

After relocating to Chicago, and within a few months of starting a new job in telecommunications sales, I happened upon a Baptist church nearby in my Logan Square neighborhood. I later learned my path was guided to this new place that would help me embark on the road to financial freedom.

At this critical juncture, I recall the inner voice of doubt attempting to dissuade me from going inside to solicit the church's telephone business. I told myself, *It's a church—they won't buy what you're selling* and *You're not going to make any money, so why bother?* Fortunately, I ignored those negative thoughts and proceeded inside where I was introduced to Angel Martinez, the church finance manager.

After some small talk, we began to discuss my sales pitch and business proposal. Within a half hour, I overcame Angel's skepticism, and he realized the value of the business proposition. After completion of the transaction, I was feeling pretty good about my sale and glad that I ignored the inner thoughts that would have prevented me from entering the church that day. As we were wrapping up, Angel asked me about my spiritual background. I was happy to share that I grew up as a Baptist church member

and had what I perceived to be a good faith-based relationship with God.

When he questioned whether I had a current church
home in the Chicago area, I told him I did not have one yet,
given that I had been in Illinois for less than six months.
While some contacts had recommended a few city churches,
I had not yet found a permanent church home that I could
relate to like I had my Texas church. Surprisingly, Angel
turned the tables and had a pitch for me...he invited me to
the upcoming Sunday church services. My initial reaction
was *Great, he just bought my services, so now I have to
buy his services*, but I accepted the invitation to come to the
next service.

That Sunday morning, I debated attending the service
because I felt I was going to be trapped into returning, even
if I didn't like the environment or the pastor. Unexpect-
edly, Pastor Lyons was as engaging and dynamic as Finance
Manager Angel Martinez had promised he would be. As it
happened, Pastor Lyons was preaching a series of sermons
focused on tithing and God's promise if his people obeyed
his word. Although I had heard versions of the message
before, I was intrigued by the speaker and I returned to hear
more. After several months under his teaching, in the fall
of 1998, I was motivated to consider accepting the pastor's
open request for his congregation to commit to the principles of tithing. As a believer who considers himself to be
as strong in faith as others in the church, even I found this
to be a big step.

Although still deep in debt, I accepted the pastor's infor-
mal invitation to commit to tithing 10 percent of my earnings for the next year. In taking the leap of faith, I found

myself asking *How is my financial situation possibly going to improve if I am giving away more of my income to the church?* I had to resist the temptation to skip Sunday services because of finances or when I was fighting skepticism because I was not "seeing" results in the time frame that I deemed necessary.

With my employment situation growing dire, the job I had started in the summer of 1998 that introduced me to my new Chicago church home was now rife with uncertainty because of industry changes. However, despite many issues of concern, I kept the faith and maintained my tithing commitment. By December 1998, I received a networking call that ultimately led to an offer for a sales recruiting opportunity and by January 1999, I had started a new higher-paying role.

Around the same time I started this new job, I received another networking call from a financial advisor who worked with a colleague from my last job. Although I was familiar with the work of financial advisors, I thought I could not afford to work with a representative and that advisors worked only with affluent clients. This advisor was early in his career but seeking to add interested clients regardless of financial status to build his client base. In working with this advisor, I learned some key strategies about effectively managing debt while starting to invest for my future. At the time, I did not think it was possible, but now I had someone willing and capable to evaluate my entire financial state and develop a short- and long-term plan to get out of debt within three years. He set up a strategic approach for debt reduction while meeting monthly budgeted expenses and, with my insistence, continuing to tithe my 10 percent every Sunday. With my new job in 1999 going well, I was blessed with a significantly higher income stream than I had ever experienced in my previous ten years of professional employment. Instead of completing my debt plan within three years, I was blessed to be debt-free within twenty-four months.

Moreover, with this newfound financial freedom, I was able to increase my regular tithing to support the church ministries, meet family financial needs, and truly start to enjoy life that comes from financial independence.

From that leap-of-faith decision regarding 10 percent tithing that I made in September 1999, my personal, professional, financial, and spiritual needs were not only met, but strengthened beyond my expectations. To this day, my personal and professional life has taken a path toward heights I never dreamed imaginable thirteen years ago when I arrived in Chicago from my downward Texas spiral. I have never returned to that short-sighted, faithless mind-set about tithing as my spiritual rewards continue to be strong, and my prayer requests continue to be answered. If I can impart any words of wisdom from my personal testimony, I urge you to take that leap of faith and tithe. For if it be his will, believe that his power will meet your needs if you ask in prayer and commit in tithes according to his word. God bless.

Sharon

I started tithing when I was a child. My mother would give me a ten-dollar allowance and explained that 10 percent belonged to God. I gave one dollar in the offering plate whenever I got my allowance. That was all I knew. I thought it was a rule, similar to stopping at stop signs. When I was old enough to get a summer job, I continued to tithe. I honestly never missed the money because I never believed it was mine.

After graduating from high school, I attended college, and my desire was to go to medical school. In my last year of college, I no longer desired to go to medical school and decided to speak with my college advisor. I was about to graduate from college and had no idea what I wanted to do after graduation. I had to decide quickly. I thank God for ordering my steps. He did it then, and he has been faithful to this day!

My advisor received a call from the University of Illinois Urbana-Champaign seeking students to study human resources. My advisor contacted me and asked if I would be interested and referred me to the advisor at the University of Illinois. I spoke with the advisor regarding graduate school. The advisor asked me to complete the application for the program, and I did. I was accepted within a week of applying and was offered a full scholarship and a job in the school's housing office. I received free housing and free meals in addition to a paycheck. God turned my situation on a dime—ten cents on a dollar—a tithe! He worked this out for me. I *know* it was because I had been faithful in my giving.

After graduating number one from the program, I was offered two jobs and took a job in New York at a great company. I have had wonderful opportunities, great international assignments, and a number of promotions. The majority of promotions I have received were not promotions that I initiated. These promotions came from God, I know. And my base salary has more than tripled since I first started in corporate America. God took me from either the wilderness to the city or the city to the wilderness in each of my moves from faith to faith and glory to glory. This last career move wasn't easy for me. In fact, it was the most difficult of them all; however, I trusted God, and I continue to walk in the direction that he guides me. This most recent opportunity has been a blessing for me, and what others have worked on for years, I received in just over a year after trusting God.

I had to carry two homes after taking this position, but God provided. I lost nothing. Everything has been a gain. I can't explain it. I do not even try to make it make sense on paper. I haven't missed a beat.

I know that my consistency in giving, which started as a child, is the reason for the elevation I've seen both professionally and financially. And I know that God can trust me with money. I give to my local church, charities, political organizations, and to others—sometimes totally on a whim. I live my life as a giver. I give finances, time, and material items. I honor my mother as the Bible says, and my family. I don't fear money. Money and possessions do not have me, I have them! I think about money as currency, and currency is from the word current. Like the current in the ocean, currency is supposed to *flow*. It is supposed to be passed from person to person. Money is not something that we are supposed to clutch and hold onto. It is something that has to be loosed.

There are times I will pay for someone's meal at a restaurant. There are times when I get this feeling I should give to people who are in need at church. I've even removed a bracelet from my wrist and given it away. You might say it's crazy. But I am simply trusting God. Tithing is an act of trust. And if you trust, you obey.

chapter 9
Scriptural References

Malachi 3:8–12 "Will a man rob God? Yet you have robbed Me! But you say, 'In what way have we robbed You?' In tithes and offerings. You are cursed with a curse, For you have robbed Me, [Even] this whole nation. Bring all the tithes into the storehouse, That there may be food in My house, And try Me now in this," says the LORD of hosts, "If I will not open for you the windows of heaven And pour out for you [such] blessing That [there will] not [be room] enough [to receive it.] And I will rebuke the devourer for your sakes, So that he will not destroy the fruit of your ground, Nor shall the vine fail to bear fruit for you in the field," says the LORD of hosts; "And all nations will call you blessed, For you will be a delightful land," says the LORD of hosts.

Proverbs 3:9–10 Honor the LORD with your possessions, And with the first fruits of all your increase; So your barns will be filled with plenty, And your vats will overflow with new wine.

Nehemiah 13:5 And he had prepared for him a large room, where previously they had stored the grain offerings, the frankincense, the articles, the tithes of grain, the new wine and oil, which were commanded [to be given] to the Levites and singers and gatekeepers, and the offerings for the priests.

Nehemiah 10:37–38 To bring the first fruits of our dough, our offerings, the fruit from all kinds of trees, [the] new wine and oil, to the priests, to the storerooms of the house of our God; and to bring the tithes of our land to the Levites, for the Levites should receive the tithes in all our farming communities. And the priest, the descendant of Aaron, shall be with the Levites when the Levites receive tithes; and the Levites shall bring up a tenth of the tithes to the house of our God, to the rooms of the storehouse.

2 Chronicles 31:12 Then they faithfully brought in the offerings, the tithes, and the dedicated things; Cononiah the Levite had charge of them, and Shimei his brother [was] the next.

1 Chronicles 29:9 Then the people rejoiced, for they had offered willingly, because with a loyal heart they had offered willingly to the LORD; and King David also rejoiced greatly.

Matthew 22:15–22 Then the Pharisees went and plotted how they might entangle Him in [His] talk. And they sent to Him their disciples with the Herodians, saying, "Teacher, we know that You are true, and teach the way of God in truth; nor do You care about anyone, for You do not regard the person of men. Tell us, therefore, what do You think? Is it lawful to pay taxes to Caesar, or not?" But Jesus perceived their wickedness, and said, "Why do you test Me, [you] hypocrites? Show Me the tax money." So they brought Him a denarius. And He said to them, "Whose image and inscription [is] this?" They said to Him, "Caesar's." And He said to them, "Render therefore to Caesar the things that are Caesar's, and to God the things that are God's." When they had heard [these words,] they marveled, and left Him and went their way.

Galatians 2:10 [They desired] only that we should remember the poor, the very thing which I also was eager to do.

2 Corinthians 9:6–8 But this [I say:] He who sows sparingly will also reap sparingly, and he who sows bountifully will also reap bountifully. [So let] each one [give] as he purposes in his heart, not grudgingly or of necessity; for God loves a cheerful giver. And God [is] able to make all grace abound toward you, that you, always having all sufficiency in all [things,] may have abundance for every good work.

1 Corinthians 9:11 If we have sown spiritual things for you, [is it] a great thing if we reap your material things?

Leviticus 27:32 And concerning the tithe of the herd or the flock, of whatever passes under the rod, the tenth one shall be holy to the LORD.

Leviticus 27:30–33 And all the tithe of the land, [whether] of the seed of the land [or] of the fruit of the tree,

[is] the Lord's. It [is] holy to the LORD. If a man wants at all to redeem [any] of his tithes, he shall add one-fifth to it. And concerning the tithe of the herd or the flock, of whatever passes under the rod, the tenth one shall be holy to the LORD. He shall not inquire whether it is good or bad, nor shall he exchange it; and if he exchanges it at all, then both it and the one exchanged for it shall be holy; it shall not be redeemed.

Proverbs 19:17: If you help the poor, you are lending to the LORD—and he will repay you!

Nehemiah 13:12 Then all Judah brought the tithe of the grain and the new wine and the oil to the storehouse.

Nehemiah 12:44 And at the same time some were appointed over the rooms of the storehouse for the offerings, the first fruits, and the tithes, to gather into them from the fields of the cities the portions specified by the Law for the priests and Levites; for Judah rejoiced over the priests and Levites who ministered.

2 Chronicles 31:5 As soon as the commandment was circulated, the children of Israel brought in abundance the first fruits of grain and wine, oil and honey and of all the produce of the field; and they brought in abundantly the tithe of everything.

Deuteronomy 14:23 And you shall eat before the LORD your God, in the place where He chooses to make His name abide, the tithe of your grain and your new wine and your oil, of the firstborn of your herds and your flocks, that you may learn to fear the LORD your God always.

Deuteronomy 14:22 You shall truly tithe all the increase of your grain that the field produces year by year.

1 Timothy 5:17–18 Let the elders who rule well be counted worthy of double honor, especially those who labor in the word and doctrine. For the Scriptures say, "You shall not muzzle an ox while it treads out the grain," and "The laborer [is] worthy of his wages."

1 Corinthians 9:7 Who ever goes to war at his own expense? Who plants a vineyard and does not eat of its fruit? Or who tends a flock and does not drink of the milk of the flock?

Luke 18:12 I fast twice a week; I give tithes of all that I possess.

Amos 4:4 Come to Bethel and transgress, At Gilgal multiply transgression; Bring your sacrifices every morning, Your tithes every three days.

Proverbs 3:9 Honor the LORD with your possessions, And with the first fruits of all your increase.

Job 41:11 Who has preceded Me, that I should pay [him?] Everything under heaven is Mine.

2 Corinthians 9:7 [So let] each one [give] as he purposes in his heart, not grudgingly or of necessity; for God loves a cheerful giver.

Deuteronomy 12:11 Then there will be the place where the LORD your God chooses to make His name abide. There you shall bring all that I command you: your burnt offerings, your sacrifices, your tithes, the heave offerings of your hand, and all your choice offerings which you vow to the LORD.

Deuteronomy 12:6 There you shall take your burnt offerings, your sacrifices, your tithes, the heave offerings of your hand, your vowed offerings, your freewill offerings, and the firstborn of your herds and flocks.

Numbers 18:28 Thus you shall also offer a heave offering to the LORD from all your tithes which you receive from the children of Israel, and you shall give the Lord's heave offering from it to Aaron the priest.

Numbers 18:24 For the tithes of the children of Israel, which they offer up [as] a heave offering to the LORD, I have given to the Levites as an inheritance; therefore I have said to them, "Among the children of Israel they shall have no inheritance."

Deuteronomy 14:22 You shall truly tithe all the increase of your seed, that the field brings forth year by year.

2 Chronicles 31:6 And concerning the children of Israel and Judah, that lived in the cities of Judah, they also brought in the tithe of oxen and sheep, and the tithe of holy things which were consecrated to the LORD their God, and laid them by heaps.

James 1:17 Every good gift and every perfect gift is from above, and comes down from the Father of lights, with whom there is no variation or shadow of turning.

Prayer

Father, I thank you for everyone who has read this book and who desires to give to the kingdom of heaven that none would suffer lack. I pray that their barns will be filled with plenty as they make that step to pay their tithes and give offerings.

I believe your word as it states that you will open the windows of heaven and pour out blessings on this reader that the reader doesn't have room enough to receive. I pray that everyone who gives receives good measure, pressed down, shaken together, and running over blessings! I pray the favor of God over every reader's life that miracles, signs, and wonders will follow him or her. I pray readers will live a debt-free life and prosper and be in good health as their souls prosper.

I pray the kingdom of heaven over their lives as there is no lack in heaven or sickness. I pray against the fear of giving and anxiety. I pray bold faith on every believer. Thy kingdom come and thy will be done on earth as it is in heaven, in Jesus's name.

REFERENCES

CNBC.com. "The Oprah Effect." *CNBC*. Last modified June 4, 2009. Accessed January 30, 2013. http://www.cnbc.com/id/29961298/The_Oprah_Effect.

Forbes.com. "World's Most Powerful People: Bill Gates." *Forbes*. Last modified December 2012. Accessed January 28, 2013. http://www.forbes.com/profile/bill-gates/.

Forbes.com. "World's Most Powerful People: Oprah Winfrey." *Forbes*. Last modified December 2012. Accessed January 28, 2013. http://www.forbes.com/profile/oprah-winfrey/.

Forbes.com. "World's Most Powerful People: Warren Buffett." *Forbes*. Last modified December 2012. Accessed January 28, 2013. http://www.forbes.com/profile/warren-buffett/.

Investopedia.com. "The Oprah Effect." *Investopedia*. Last modified April 14, 2010. Accessed January 30, 2013. http://www.investopedia.com/financial-edge/0410/the-oprah-effect.

Jewfaq.com. "Judaism 101." *JewFaq*. Last modified 1995–2011. Accessed February 1, 2013. http://jewfaq.org/tzedakah.htm.

The Holy Bible, King James Version.(Pure Cambridge edition) 1611 King James Bible Online, 2013. http:www. kingjamesbibleonline.org.

New International Version Bible. BibleGateway Online 2013. http:www.biblegateway.com.

Philanthropy.com. "Corporate Giving Slow to Recover as Economy Remains Shaky." *The Chronicles of Philanthropy.* Last modified July 14, 2011. Accessed January 30, 2013. http://philanthropy.com/article/Big-Business-Won.

You May Contact

Cynthia Dickens by:

E-mail: info@beacheerfulgivercd.com

Web site: www.beacheerfulgivercd.com

Made in the USA
Charleston, SC
06 August 2013